Wolfgang Amadeus

MOZART

Mass in C minor

K. 427 (417a)

Reconstruction by
Alois Schmitt

Vocal Score
Klavierauszug

SERENISSIMA MUSIC, INC.

CONTENTS

I. KYRIE

(Source: Composer's fair-copy full score, K. 427)

II. GLORIA

(Source: Composer's fair-copy full score, K. 427)

III. CREDO

IV. SANCTUS

(Source: Composer's fair-copy full score, K. 427)

V. AGNUS DEI

ORCHESTRA

2 Flutes, 2 Oboes, 2 Clarinets, 2 Bassoons
2 Horns, 2 Trumpets, 4 Trombones
Timpani, Organ
Violin I, Violin II, Viola, Violoncello, Double Bass

Duration: ca. 80 minutes
First performance: April 3, 1901
Martin Luther Kirche, Dresden
Soli, Chorus and Orchestra / Alois Schmitt

Complete orchestral parts compatible with this vocal score are available (Cat. No. A2699) from
E. F. Kalmus & Co., Inc.
6403 West Rogers Circle
Boca Raton, FL 33487 USA
(800) 434 - 6340
www.kalmus-music.com

PREFACE

Mozart worked on the *Mass in C minor, K. 427* during the years 1782-1783. His plan was to perform it in his native city of Salzburg after his marriage to Constanze set for August 4, 1782. However, the composition was still unfinished by the autumn of 1783. In order to keep his promise, Mozart performed the completed movements of the Mass, with Konstanze as one of the soprano soloists, in the church of St. Peter's convent on October 26, 1783. He most likely filled in the missing sections of the mass in with earlier pieces, as was common practice at the time. Since there are no longer any records of the nature and extent of these alterations, the *Mass in C minor, K. 427* has come down to us only as a fragment.

The *Mass in C minor* was edited and completed from 1897 to 1901 by the conductor of the Mozartverein, Alois Schmitt. He was encouraged and assisted in this endeavor by Ernst Lewicki, the co-founder, and later, chairman of the Mozartverein in Dresden. Inspired by Franz Xaver Süssmayr's work in completing Mozart's *Requiem, K. 626*, Schmitt followed Mozart's sketches to complete the instrumentation. Like Süssmayr, he created an organ part and constructed the final "Agnus Dei" from the opening "Kyrie." Unlike Süssmayr, who composed new material to fill in missing sections of a fragmentary original, Schmitt provided for the missing portions of the Credo by borrowing movements from the composer's earlier liturgical works.

On April 3rd and 5th of 1901, Alois Schmitt conducted the first performance of his completed version of the work in the Martin Luther Kirche in Dresden. Although Schmitt's reconstruction was later repeatedly subjected to criticism, it has amply proven itself in performance countless times over the past century. Schmitt's highly sensitive and experienced hand is revealed throughout its pages.

In his own preface to the first edition of the score, Schmitt provides some information about the origins of the Mass and gives the reader his general view of the work:

> Mozart could complete neither of his most important compositions in the genre of church music; the great C-minor Mass and the Requiem. In the latter case, death stilled his hand. In the former, the work remained unfinished due to a series of unfortunate circumstances.
>
> Mozart began writing the Mass in order to keep a promise which he had made to his father, namely that he would compose a great mass and perform it in Salzburg. Given Mozart's early experiences arranging Bach fugues and Handel oratorios for Baron van Swieten, it is not surprising that the influence of North German Protestant art is pervasive in this Mass. The Credo and Sanctus recall Handel, and the Gloria even mimics note for note a passage from the *Hallelujah Chorus* from Handel's *Messiah*. The quartet Benedictus is more in the spirit of Bach. The austere sweetness and masterful polyphony have a unique flavor not to be found anywhere else in Mozart. Mozart's ability to adjust quickly from one style to another is quite astonishing.

When the young couple arrived in Salzburg in July 1783, only the Kyrie, Gloria, Sanctus and Benedictus were completed. The Credo was only partly written, and the Agnus Dei not yet begun. The first performance was held at St. Peter's in Salzburg on August 25 [The actual date was October 26.]

Mozart would hardly have contented himself with the fragment for the Salzburg performance. He most likely filled in the missing sections with counterparts from earlier Masses (of which he had already written sixteen).

Upon his return to Vienna, Mozart was so busy with teaching and preparing his numerous musical academy concerts that he found no time to compose church music. Requested to write an Italian oratorio in a few weeks time for a charity concert during Lent, the ever-obliging master took up the offer. However, unable to compose a new work of such dimensions in so short a time, he turned to his incomplete Mass and extracted more than half of its music for the oratorio. An Italian text [by Lorenzo Da Ponte] was underlaid more or less successfully. Two newly-composed arias and a three-part cadence for the closing fugue of the Gloria were added. Thus was born the occasional oratorio *Davidde Penitente, K. 469* which was first performed on March 13 and 17, 1785. The fate of the *Mass, K. 427* was thus sealed. It remained incomplete despite the fragment that was first published in 1840.

The completed Sanctus and Benedictus, which were not utilized in the oratorio, and the two incomplete Credo parts were not taken into consideration. Mozart did not reach the sublime gravity and deeply religious solemnity of this great C-minor Mass in any of his other works apart from *Requiem*, also unfinished. The intense writing, the use of five and eight part choral textures, the broad disposition of each movement and the treatment of the orchestra, all raise this Mass to a level far beyond Mozart's earlier efforts in the genre.

May 1901 ALOIS SCHMITT

Mass in C minor

K. 427 (417a)

1. Kyrie

Wolfgang Amadeus Mozart

Reconstruction by Alois Schmitt

SERENISSIMA MUSIC, INC.

Z269991

Masters Music Publications, Inc., Sole Selling Agent

11
lei - - - son, e - - lei - - - - - - son, Ky - ri - e - e -
Ky - - -
11
14
lei - son, e - lei - son, e - lei - son, e - lei - son, e - lei - son, e - lei -
- - ri - e e - lei - - - son, e - lei - - - - - -
14
17
A
son, e - lei - - - - - - son, e - lei - - son, e -
son, e - lei - - son. Ky - ri - e,
Ky - - - - ri - e e -
Ky - ri - e — e - lei - son, e - lei - son, e -
17
A

20
lei - - son, e - lei - - - - - - - son, e - lei - - -
Ky - ri - e e - - lei - son, Ky - - ri - e e -
lei - - son, e - lei - - - - - - - son, e - lei - son, e -
lei - son, e - lei - son, e - lei - son, e - lei - son, e - lei - son, e - lei - son,
20
23
- - - son, e - lei - - - son, Ky - ri - e e - -
lei - - - - - - - son, Ky - ri - e e - -
lei - son, e - lei - son, Ky - - - ri - e e - -
e - lei - son, e - lei - son, Ky - - ri - e
23
25
lei - - - - - - - son. Ky - - ri -
lei - - - - - - - son. Ky - - ri -
lei - - - - - - - son. Ky - - ri -
e - lei - - - - son. Ky - - ri -
p
25

28
e e - lei - son, e - lei - son, e - lei - son, e -
e e - lei
e e - lei - son, e - lei
e e - lei - son, e -
31
lei - son.
son.
son.
le - i - son.
Vl.
Ob. Fag.
34 B
SOLO Soprano
Chri - ste e - lei - son, e - lei - son,
TUTTI Sopr.
p
Alt
Chri -
TUTTI
e - lei -
e - lei -
p

38
Chri - - ste, Chri - ste - e - lei - - -
tr
ste,
son,
son,
38
42
son, e - lei - - - - - - - - -
p
Chri - - ste, Chri_ste
p
Chri - - - - - - - ste
p
Chri - - - - - - ste
42
46
cresc.
- son, e - lei_son, e - lei_son, e - lei - - son.
f
p
e_lei_son, e_lei_son, e_lei - son.
cresc.
f
e_lei_son, e_lei_son, e_lei - son.
cresc.
f
e_lei_son, e_lei_son, e_lei - son.
cresc.
f
46
cresc.
f
p

51
SOLO Soprano
Chri - - - ste, Chri-ste e - lei - - son,
p
f
55
p
Chri - ste, Chri - - ste e - lei - - son, e -
59
lei - son, e - - - lei - son, e - - - lei - - - -
62
tr
- son,
TUTTI Soprano
p
e - - lei - son, e - - - lei - son, Chri-ste e -
SOLO
Alt
Chri - - ste e - - lei - son.
Tenor
e - - - lei - - - - - - - son.
Bass
e - - lei - - - - - - - son.
62

65 SOLO Soprano
tr
lei
68
71
TUTTI Soprano
f
son.
Ky - ri - e e - lei - son, Ky -
74
- ri - e e - lei - son, e - lei - - son, e -
TUTTI
e - lei - son, e - lei - son,
TUTTI
Ky - ri - e e -

77
lei - son, e - lei - - son, e - lei - - son, e -
Ky - ri - e, Ky - ri - e, Ky - ri - e e -
lei - son, Ky - - - ri - e e - lei - - son, e -
TUTTI
f
Ky - ri - e e - lei - son, e - lei - son, e - lei - son, e - lei - son,
77
tr
80
lei - - - son, e - lei - - - son, e - lei - - -
lei - son, Ky - ri - e e - lei - - - son, e -
lei - - - son, e - lei - son, e - lei - son, e - lei - son, e -
e - lei - son, e - lei - son, e - lei - son, e - lei - son, e - lei - son, e - lei - son,
80
83
- - son, Ky - ri - e e - lei - - son.
lei - - son, Ky - ri - e e - lei - - son.
lei - son, e - lei - - - son.
e - lei - son, Ky - ri - e e - lei - - son.
83

86
D
Ky - ri - e e - lei - son, e - lei - son, e -
Ky - ri - e e - lei - son,
Ky - ri - e e - le - i -
Ky - ri - e e - lei - son,
86
D
89
lei - son, e - lei - son, e - lei - son,
Ky - ri - e e - lei - son,
son, Ky - ri - e e - lei - son,
Ky - ri - e e - le - i - son,
89
(91)
e - le - i - son.
e - le - i - son.
e - le - i - son.
e - le - i - son.
(91)

2. Gloria

Allegro vivace
Soprano
Alto
Tenor
Bass
Piano
TUTTI
Glo - ri - a
in ex - cel - sis, in ex - cel
sis, Glo - ri - a in ex -
in ex - cel - sis,

10
De_o, Glo_ _ _ _ _ _ _ _ ri_a in ex_cel_sis, Glo_ _ri_a in ex_
cel_sis, Glo_ _ _ _ _ ri_a in ex_cel_sis, Glo_
cel_sis, Glo_ _ri_a in ex_cel_sis, in ex_
in ex_cel_ _ _ _ _ _ _ _sis De_o,
13
celsis, in ex_celsis, in ex_celsis, in ex_cel_ _ _ _ _ _ _ _sis
_ri_a in ex_celsis, in ex_celsis, in ex_cel_ _ _ _ _ _sis,
celsis, in ex_celsis, in ex_cel_ _ _ _ _ _sis,
Glo_ _ri_a in ex_celsis, in ex_celsis, in ex_cel_ _ _ _ _
16 A
De_ _ _ _ _ _ _ _ _ _o, in ex_cel_ _ _
in ex_cel_ _ _ _ _ _sis De_o, in ex_cel_ _ _
in ex_cel_ _ _ _ _ _sis De_o, in ex_
sis, in ex_cel_ _ _ _ _sis De_o, in ex_

19
- - - - sis De_o, in excel_sis, in ex_cel_sis, in excel_sis,
- - - - sis De_o, in excel_sis, in ex_cel_sis, in excel_sis,
cel - - - - - sis De_o, in excel_sis, in ex_cel_sis, in excel_sis,
cel _ sis De _ - - o, in excel_sis, in ex_cel_sis, in excel_sis,
19
22
p
et in ter - - ra, in ter - ra pax ho - mi - nibus
p
et in ter - ra, in ter - ra pax ho - mi - nibus
p
et in ter - ra pax ho - mi - nibus
p
et in ter - - ra pax ho - mi - nibus
22
p
p
27
bo - - - - - nae vo - - - - -
bo - - - - - nae
bo - - - - -
27
fp

30
lun - ta -
vo - lun - ta -
nae vo - lun - ta -
bo - nae vo - lun -
30
33
B
f
tis. Glo - ri-a in ex - cel-sis, in excel-sis, in ex-
tis. Glo - ri-a in excel - sis, in ex-
tis. Glo - ri-a in excel-sis, in ex - cel-sis, in ex-cel-sis, in ex-
ta - tis. Glo - ri-a in ex-
33
B
36
celsis, in ex-cel - sis De -
celsis, in ex-cel - sis, in ex-cel -
cel - sis, in ex-cel -
cel-sis, in ex-cel-sis, in ex - cel - sis, in ex-
36

o, in ex_cel - sis
sis De_o, in ex_cel - sis
sis De_o, in ex _ cel - sis
cel - sis De_o, in ex _ cel _ sis De -
De_o, in excel_sis, in ex_cel_sis, in excel_sis, et in ter -
De_o, in excel_sis, in ex_cel_sis, in excel_sis, et in
De_o, in excel_sis, in ex_cel_sis, in excel_sis,
o, in excel_sis, in ex_cel_sis, in excel_sis, et in
C
p
ra, in ter - ra pax ho - mi - nibus bo -
ter - ra, in ter - ra pax ho - mi - nibus
et in ter - ra pax ho - mi - nibus
ter - ra pax ho - mi - nibus
fp

50
nae vo - - - - - - lun - - - - - -
bo - - - - - - nae vo - - - - - -
bo - - - - - - nae
bo - - - - - -
50
53
ta - - - - - - - - - - - - tis.
lun - - - - ta - - - - - - - - tis.
vo - lun - ta - - - - - - - - - tis.
- nae vo - lun - ta - - - - tis.
53
p
57
pp

3. Laudamus Te

B
te,
a - - - - - do -
ra - mus te,
glo - ri - fi - ca - mus te
glo - ri - fi -
ca - - - - - - - - - - - - - - -
mus
NB.

45
C
te, glo_ri_fi _ ca _
tr
tr
50
tr
mus
cresc.
54
te.
f
tr
57
D
Lau da _ mus
Ob.
p
61
te, a_do_ra_ _mus te. Be ne_ di_ _cimus

66
te, glo-ri-fi-ca-mus te, glo-ri- -fi-ca-mus te, lau-damus
Ob
fp
fp
fp
fp
72
te, a-do-ra-mus te.
fp
mfp
f
76
E
Lau-da-
p
tr
tr
tr
81
-mus te,
be-ne-
f
p
86
di-ci-mus te,
be-ne-di-ci-mus
f
p

91
F
te,
a - do -
94
ra - mus te,
glo - ri - fi - ca -
98
102
107
G
NB
- mus te,

112
glo - ri - fi - ca
tr
116
H
mus te, glo - ri - fi -
fp
fp
fp
120
ca
mus
p
cresc.
124
te.
tr
f
127

4. Gratias

Adagio
Soprano I
Soprano II
Alto
Tenor
Bass
Piano
Gra - ti-as, gra - ti-as a-gimus ti - bi propter magnam, ma - gnam
Gra - ti-as a - gimus ti - bi propter ma - gnam, ma - gnam
Gra - ti-as a - gimus ti - bi pro - pter ma - gnam, ma - gnam
Gra - ti-as a - gimus ti - bi pro - pter ma - gnam, ma - gnam
Gra - tias a - gimus ti - bi pro - pter, pro - pter ma - gnam, ma - gnam

5
glo - ri-am tu - - - - - am, gra - - - ti -
p
7
as a - - - gi - mus pro - - - pter ma - gnam
f

9
glo - riam, pro - - - pter ma - gnam glo - ri - am tu - - -
pro - - - pter ma - gnam glo - ri - am tu - - -
glo - riam, pro - - - pter ma - gnam glo - ri - am tu - - -
glo - riam, pro - - - pter ma - gnam glo - ri - am tu - - -
glo - riam, pro - - - pter ma - gnam glo - ri - am tu - - -
9
11
am.
am.
am.
am.
am.
11

5. Domine

Allegro moderato
Piano
f
tr
6
p
f
11
Soprano
Do - mine De - us
16
rex coe - le - stis, rex coe - le - stis, De -
21
us pa - ter, De - us pa - ter

26
A
o - mni po - tens.
Mezzosopran
Do - mi-ne fi - li u - - - ni - ge - ni-te
A
tr
31
Je - su Chri-ste Do - - mi - ne De - us. A - - -
36
gnus De - - - - i fi - li-us, fi - li-us
41
Do - mine fi - li u - ni - ge - ni-te
pa - - tris, Do - mine De - - us rex coe -
tr

46
B
Je - su, Je - - - - - - su Chri - ste.
le - - stis De - - us pa - ter o - mnipotens.
B
f
51
tr
tr
tr
tr
56
tr
Do - mi-ne De - us, Do - - mine De - us, A - - -
Do - mine De - us, Do - - mi-ne De - us, A - - -
p
61
gnus De - - - - - i fi - li-us,
gnus De - - - - - i fi - li-us,

65
fi - li_us pa - - - - tris, A_gnus De_i
fi - li_us pa - - - - tris, fi_li_us
69 C
fi - - li_us pa - - - - tris,
pa - - - - - - - - - - - - - - - -
C
73
fi - - li_us, fi - lius pa - - - - tris,
- - - - - - - tris, fi - li_us pa - - tris, A_gnus
77
fi_li_us pa - - - - - - - - - - - - -
De_i fi - - - li_us pa - - - -

81
tris,
A
85
tris,
fi - li_us, fi - li - us pa - tris,
gnus De_i fi - li_us pa - tris,
90
fi_li_us,
fi - li_us pa -
fi_li_us,
fi - li_us pa -
tr
tr
f
p
96
tris.
tris.
f
tr

6. Qui Tollis

Largo
Soprano
Alto
Tenor
Bass
Soprano
Alto
Tenor
Bass
Piano
Qui tol - - lis pec - ca - ta mun - - di,
Qui tol - - lis pec - ca - ta mun - - di,
Qui tol - - lis pec - ca - ta mun - - di,
Qui tol - - lis pec - ca - ta mun - - di,
Qui tol - - - lis
Qui tol - -
Qui tol - -
Qui tol - -

7
qui tol - lis pec - cæ - ta, qui
qui tol - - lis, qui
qui tol - lis pec - ca - ta, qui
qui tol - - lis, qui tol - -
7
— pec - ca - ta mun - - di, qui
lis pec - ca - ta mun - - di, qui
lis pec - ca - ta mun - - di, qui tol - lis,
lis pec - ca - ta mun - - di, qui
7
10
tol - lis, qui tol - lis pec - ca
tol - lis, qui tol - lis, qui tol - - - - -
tol - lis, qui tol - lis, qui tol - -
- lis pec - ca - - - - ta mun - - di, pec - -
10
tol - lis, qui tol - lis pec - ca - - - - -
tol - lis, qui tol - lis pec - - ca - - ta,
qui tol - lis pec - ca - ta mun - - di,
tol - lis pec - ca - ta mun - - di, pec - -
10

13
A
p
- - - - ta mun - - - - di, mi - se - re -
lis pec - ca - ta mun - - - - di,
lis pec - ca - ta mun - - - - di,
ca - - - - ta mun - - - - - di,
ta, pec - ca - ta mun - - - - di,
pec - ca - ta mun - - - - di,
pec - ca - ta mun - - - - di,
ca - - - - ta mun - - - - - di,
pp
16
f
- re, mi - se - re-re no - bis, qui
mi - se - re-re no - bis,
mi - se - re-re no - bis,
mi - se - re-re no - bis,
mi - se - re- - re, mi - - se-rere no - bis,
mi - - se-rere no - bis,
mi - - se-rere no - bis,
mi - - se-rere no - bis,

tol - - lis pec - ca - ta mun - - di,
qui tol - - lis pec - ca - ta mun - - di,
qui tol - - lis pec - ca - ta mun - - di,
qui tol - - lis pec - ca - ta mun - - di,
qui tol - lis pec -
qui tol -
qui tol - lis pec -
qui tol -
qui tol - lis, qui tol - lis
qui tol - lis, qui tol - lis pec - ca - ta,
qui tol - lis, qui tol - lis pec - ca -
qui tol - lis pec - ca - ta mun -
ca - ta, qui tol - lis, qui tol - lis,
lis, qui tol - lis, qui tol - lis, qui
ca - ta, qui tol - lis, qui tol - lis pec -
lis, qui tol - - lis pec - ca - - ta mun -

25
B
p
qui tol - lis pec - ca - ta mun -
qui tol - lis pec - ca - ta mun -
ta mun - di, pec - ca - ta mun -
di, pec - ca - ta mun -
25
qui tol - lis pec - ca - ta mun -
tol - lis pec - ca - ta mun -
ca - ta, qui tol - lis pec - ca - ta mun -
di, pec - ca - ta mun -
25
B
28
di. Su - sci - pe, su - scipe, su - scipe depre -
di. Su - scipe depre -
di. Su - scipe depre -
di. Su - scipe depre -
28
di. Su - sci - pe, su - scipe, su -
di. Su - sci - pe, su - scipe, su -
di. Su - sci - pe, su - scipe, su -
di. Su - sci - pe, su - scipe,
28
pp

31
ca - - - ti - o - nem no - - stram, qui se - - - des
ca - ti - o - - nem no - - stram, qui se -
ca - ti - o - nem no - - stram, qui se -
ca - ti - o - nem no - - stram, qui se -
31
scipe depre - ca - ti - onem no - - stram,
scipe depre - ca - ti - onem no - - stram,
scipe depre - ca - ti - onem no - - stram,
suscipe depre - ca - ti - onem no - - stram,
31
f
f
34
ad de - xte - ram pa - - tris, qui se - des
des ad de - xte - ram pa - - tris, qui se - des
des ad de - xte - ram pa - - tris, qui se - des
des ad de - xte - ram pa - - tris, qui se - des
34
qui se - des, qui se - des ad
qui se - - - - - - -
qui se - - - des, qui se - - -
qui se - - - des, qui se - - -
34

37
ad dexteram pa - tris, qui se - des, qui
ad dexteram pa - tris, qui se - des, qui se - des
ad dexteram pa - tris, qui se - des, qui
ad dexteram pa - tris, qui se - des ad
37
dexte-ram pa - - - tris, qui se - des, qui
des ad dexteram pa - tris, qui se - des, qui
des ad dexteram pa - tris, qui se - des, qui
des ad dexteram pa - tris, qui se - - - - des ad de - -
37
40
se - des, qui se - - - - - des ad de - xteram
ad de - xteram, qui se - - des ad de - xteram
se - des, qui se - - - des ad de - xteram
dexte - ram pa - - tris, qui se - des ad de - xteram
40
se - des, qui se - - des ad de - xteram
se - des, qui se - - des, qui se - des ad de - xteram
se - des, qui se - des, qui se - des ad de - xteram
- - xteram pa - - tris, qui se - des ad de - xteram
40

43
C
pa - - tris, mi - se - re - re,
pa - - tris, mi - se - re - re,
pa - - tris, mi - se - re - re,
pa - - tris, mi - se - re - re,
43
pa - - tris, mi - se - re-
pa - - tris, mi - se - re-
pa - - tris, mi - se - re-
pa - - tris, mi - se - re-
43
C
46
mi - se-rere nobis, misere - re,
mi - se-rere nobis, misere - re,
mi - se-rere nobis, misere - re,
mi - se-rere nobis, misere - re,
46
- re, mi - se-rere no-bis, mi-se-
- re, mi - se-rere no-bis, mi-se-
- re, mi - se-rere no-bis, mi-se-
- re, mi - se-rere no-bis, mi-se-
46

49
mi-sere - re, mi-sere - re no - - - - bis, mi-se -
mi-sere - re, mi-sere - re no - - - - bis, mi-se -
mi-sere - re, mi-sere - re no - - - - bis, mi-se -
mi-sere - re, mi-sere - re no - - - - bis, mi-se -
49
re - re, mi-se- re - re, mise- re - re no- - bis, mi-se -
re - re, mi-se- re - re, mise- re - re no- - bis, mi-se -
re - re, mi-se- re - re, mise- re - re no- - bis, mi-se -
re - re, mi-se- re - re, mise- re - re no- - bis, mi-se -
49
p
53
re - - re no - - - - - bis.
re - - re no - - - - - bis.
re - - re no - - - - - bis.
re - - re no - - - - - bis.
53
re - - re no - - - - - bis.
re - - re no - - - - - bis.
re - - re no - - - - - bis.
re - - re no - - - - - bis.
53
pp

7. Quoniam

Allegro
Piano
A Soprano
Quo - - ni-
Mezzo Soprano
Quo - ni-am tu so - - - - - lus san - ctus,
Tenor
A

28
am tu so - - - - - - - lus Do - mi - nus, — tu —
tu so_lus san - - - - - - - - - - - - - ctus, tu so_lus
Quo - - ni - am tu
28
34
so - - - - lus tu so - - - - lus Do - minus,
san - - - - - - - - - - ctus, tu so - - - - lus
so - - - - - lus al - tis - - si_mus, tu so -
34
40
tu so - - - - - - - - lus Do - - mi - nus,
san - ctus, tu so - - - - - - - lus san - - - ctus,
- - - - - - lus al - tis - - si - mus, quo - - - ni-
40

45
quo - - ni - am, quo - - ni - am tu so - lus san - - -
quo - - ni - am tu so - - lus
am tu
45
50
- - - - - - - - - - - - - ctus, tu so - - -
sanctus, tu so - - lus, so - lus san - - - - - - -
so - - lus sanctus, Do - minus tu, tu so - lus al -
B
50
B
55
- - lus san - - - - - - - - - - - - -
- - - - - - ctus, tu so - lus san - - - - - - - -
tis - - si - mus, tu so - lus san - - - - - - - - - -
55

ctus,
ctus,
ctus,
f
tu so - lus Do - mi - nus, tu so - lus al -
tu so - lus Do - mi - nus, tu so - lus al -
tu so - lus Do - mi - nus, tu so - lus al -
p
p
cresc.
tis - si - mus.
tis - si - mus.
tis - si - mus.
C
f

77
Quo_
83
_ ni _ am tu so_lus san _ _ ctus, tu so_lus san _ ctus, quo_
Quo _ ni _ am tu so_lus san _ ctus, tu solus
Quo _ ni _ am tu solus
89
_ ni _ am tu solus san _
sanctus, quo _ ni _ am tu solus san _
sanctus, quo _ ni _ am tu so_lus

95 D
san
ctus, tu so_lus san ctus, tu so_lus
ctus, tu so_lus san ctus, tu so_lus
100
105
san ctus. Quo_ ni_am tu so_lus, tu so_
san_ ctus. Quo_ ni_am tu so_lus,
ctus. Quo_ ni_am tu so_lus,
f
p

111
- - - - lus sanctus,
tu so - - - - - - lus sanctus,
tu
118
E
tu so - - - - - - - - - - - - - -
tu so - - - - - - - - - - - - -
so - - - - - - - - - - - - - - - -
125
- lus san - ctus. Quo - ni-
- lus san - ctus. Quo - ni-am
- lus san - ctus. Quo - ni-am,

131
am tu so_lus san
tu so_lus san
quo_ni_am tu so_lus sanctus, Do_mi
131
137
ctus, tu so_lus san
nus al tis si_mus, tu so_lus san
137
142
142

147
F
ctus, tu so - lus Do - - mi - nus,
ctus, tu so - lus Do - - mi - nus,
ctus, tu so - lus Do - - mi - nus,
f
p
152
tu so - - lus al - tis - - - si - mus, al - tis - si -
tu so - - lus al - tis - - - si - mus, al - tis - si -
tu so - - lus al - tis - - - si - mus, al - tis - si -
p
157
mus, al - tis - si - mus.
mus, al - tis - si - mus.
mus, al - tis - si - mus.
f

162
167
8. Jesu Christe
Adagio
Soprano
Alto
Tenor
Bass
Piano
Je - su, Je - su Chri - - ste, Jesu Chri -
Je - su, Je - - - - su Christe, Jesu Chri -
Je - su, Je su Chri - ste, Je - su Chri -
Je - su, Je - su Chri - ste, Jesu Chri -
4
ste, Je - su Chri - ste, Je - su Chri - - - ste.
ste, Je - su Chri - ste, Je - su Chri - - - ste.
ste, Je - su Chri - ste, Je - su Chri - - - ste.
ste, Je - su Chri - ste, Je - su Chri - - - ste.
attacca

Cum Sancto Spiritu

27
cto spi - ri - tu in glo -
ri-a De-i
ri-a De-i pa - tris a -
men, a - men, a -
27
32
ri-a De-i pa-tris a - men, a -
pa - tris a - men.
men, a - men,
men, a - men, a - men. Cum san -
32
37
men, a -
Cum san - cto
a -
cto spi - ri - tu in
37

42
B
men, a
spi - ri - tu in glo - ri_a De_i pa - tris
men. Cum
glo - ri_a De_i pa - tris.
42
B
47
a
san - cto spi - ri
a
47
52
p
f
men, a - men, a
men, a - men, a
tu in glo - ri_a De_i pa
men, a - men, a
52

57
men. Cum san - - - -
men, a - - - - - men, a - - -
tris, a - - - - - - men, a - - - - - - -
men. Cum san -
57
63
- - - - cto spi - ri - tu in glo -
- - - - men, a - - - - men, a - - -
- - - - men, a - - - - - - - - - - - men,
- - - - - - - - - cto spi - ri - tu in glo -
63
68 C
men, a - - - - - - - - - - - - -
a - - men, a - - men, a - - -
- ri - a De - i pa - tris, a - - - - -
68 C

73
ria De - i patris, a - men,
men, a - men,
men, a - men, a -
men, a -
p cresc.
78
a - men, a -
a - men,
men.
Cum
men.
Cum san -
83
a -
san - cto spi - ri -
cto spi - ri - tu in

88
D
men, a
men.
tu in glo_ri_a De_i pa_tris, a_ men, a_men, a
glo_ri_a De_i pa_tris a_ men a
88
D
93
men,
Cum san
men, a men,
men, a
93
98
a men, a
cto spi ri tu in glo
a
98

103
men, a
men.
ri-a De-i pa
tris.
Cum
men, a
men. Cum san
103
108
Cum
san
cto
spi
ri
cto
spi
ri
tu, a
108
113 E
san
cto
spi
ri
tu, a
men.
Cum
san
men.
113 E

118
tu a - - - - - - - - - - - - - - -
- - - men.
cto spi - - ri - tu, cum san - - -
Cum san - - - - - - - - - - - -
118
123
- - - - - - - - - - - - - - - men.
Cum
- - - - - - - - cto spi - - ri - tu,
cto spi - - ri - tu a - - - - - - -
123
128
Cum san - - - - - - - - -
san - - - - - - - - - - cto spi - - ri -
- - - - - - - - - - - - - - - - - -
128

133
cto spi - - ri - tu in glo - - - - - - -
tu in glo - - - - - - - - - - - ri-
- - - - - - - - - - - - - - - - -
133
138 F
- ri_a. Cum san - - - - - -
a,
cum san - - - - - - - - - cto
men.
138 F
143
- - - cto spi - - ri - tu,
a - - - men.
spi - - ri - tu,
Cum san - - -
143

148
Cum san - cto
a -
cto spi - ri - tu
148
153
a - men, a -
spi - ri - tu a - men, a -
men, a - men, a -
a - men a men, a -
153
158
158

163
G
- - - - men, a - men, a - men, a - men. Cum san -
men, a - men, a - men, a - men. Cum
men, a - men, a - men.
men, a - - - - men, a - men.
163
G
169
- - - - cto spi - - - - ri - tu in glo -
san - - - - - - cto spi - ri - tu
Cum san - - - cto, cum sancto spi - ri - tu
Cum san - - - cto spi - ri - tu
169
176
in glo - - ri - a, in glo - - ri - a,
in glo - - ri - a, in glo - - ri - a,
in glo - - ri - a, in glo -
176

181
ri‑a De‑i pa‑
in glo‑ ri‑a De‑i pa‑
in glo ri‑a De‑i pa‑
ri‑a, in glo‑ ri‑a De‑i pa‑
181
186 H
tris, a‑
tris, a‑
tris, a‑
tris, a‑
186 H
191
men, a‑men, a‑men, a‑men, a‑men, a‑men.
men, a‑men, a‑men, a‑men, a‑men.
men, a‑men, a‑men, a‑men, a‑men.
men, a‑men, a‑men, a‑men, a‑men.
191

9. Credo

Allegro maestoso
Piano
Str.
Bls.
tr
Soprano I
Cre - do, cre-do in u-num De - um,
Soprano II
Cre - do, cre-do in u-num De - um,
Alto
Cre - do, cre-do in u-num De - um,
Tenor
Cre - do, cre-do in u-num De - um,
Bass
Cre - do, cre-do in u-num De - um,

17
patrem omni - poten - tem, facto - rem coe - li et ter - - -
patrem omni - poten - tem, facto - rem coe - li et ter - - -
patrem omni - poten - tem, facto - rem coe - li et ter - - -
patrem omni - poten - tem, facto - rem coe - li et ter - - -
patrem omni - poten - tem, facto - rem coe - li et ter - - -
17
21
A
rae, fa - ctorem coeli et ter - - rae, vi - si - bi - lium o - mni - um, et in -
rae, fa - ctorem coeli et ter - - rae, vi - si - bi - lium o - mni - um,
rae, fa - ctorem coeli et ter - - rae, vi - si - bi - lium o - mni - um,
rae, fa - ctorem coeli et ter - - rae, vi - si - bi - lium o - mni - um,
rae, fa - ctorem coeli et ter - - rae, vi - si - bi - lium o - mni - um,
21
A

25
vi - - - - si - - - - bi - - - - li - um,
et in - vi - - - - si - - - - bi - - - - li
et in -
et in - vi - - - - - - -
et in - vi - - - -
25
29
et in - vi - si - bi - - li - um.
um, et in - vi - si - bi - - li - um.
vi - - - - - si - bi - - li - um.
- - - - - - si - bi - - li - um.
- - - - - si - bi - li - um.
29
p

33
Cre - do
Cre - do
Cre - do
Cre - do
Cre - do
33
cresc.
f
37
et in u - num Do - mi - num,
Jesum Christum fi - li - um,
et in u - num Do - mi - num,
Jesum Christum fi - li - um,
et in u - num Do - mi - num,
Jesum Christum fi - li - um,
et in u - num Do - mi - num,
Jesum Christum fi - li - um,
et in u - num Do - mi - num,
Jesum Christum fi - li - um,
37

41
B
fi - lium De - i u - ni - ge - ni - tum, et ex pa - tre natum an -
fi - lium De - i u - ni - ge - ni - tum, et ex pa - tre na - tum an -
fi - lium De - i u - ni - ge - ni - tum, et ex pa - tre na - tum
fi - lium De - i u - ni - ge - ni - tum, et ex pa - tre na - tum
fi - lium De - i u - ni - ge - ni - tum, et ex pa - tre na - tum,
41
B
45
te,
an - te,
an - te, an -
cre - do, cre - do, cre - do, cre - do,
45

49
te omni_a sae - cu - la,
an - te omni_a sae - cu - la,
an - te omni_a sae - cu - la,
te omni_a sae - cu - la,
an - te omni_a sae - cu - la,
49
53
53

57
C
De - um de De - o,
De - um de De - o,
De - um de De - o,
De - um de De - o,
De - um de De - o,
57
C
61
lu - men de lu - mi-ne, De - um ve - rum de De-o
lu - men de lu - mi-ne, De - um ve - rum de De-o
lu - men de lu - mi-ne, De - um ve - rum de De-o
lu - men de lu - mi-ne, De - um
lu - men de lu - mi-ne, De - um
61

65
ve - - - - - ro, ge - nitum non fa - ctum,
ve - - - - - ro, ge - nitum non fa - ctum,
ve - - - - - ro, ge - nitum non fa - ctum,
ve - rum de Deo ve - - - ro, ge - nitum non fa - ctum,
ve - rum de Deo ve - - - ro, ge - nitum non fa - ctum,
65
69
D
ge - nitum non fa - ctum, con - - sub -
ge - nitum non fa - ctum, con - - -
ge - nitum non fa - ctum, con - - -
ge - nitum non fa - ctum, con - - sub - stan - ti - alem
ge - nitum non fa - ctum, con - substanti - a - - lem
69
D

73
stan - ti - alem pa - tri, per quem o -
sub - stan - ti - alem pa - tri, per quem o -
sub - stan - ti - alem pa - tri, per
pa - tri, per quem o -
pa - tri, per quem
73
77
quem o
o
77

81
mnia fa cta sunt.
mnia fa cta sunt.
mnia fa cta sunt.
mnia fa cta sunt.
mnia fa cta sunt.
81
85
Cre do, qui pro pter nos ho mi
Cre do, qui pro pter nos ho mi
Cre do, qui pro pter nos ho mi
Cre do, qui pro pter nos ho mi
Cre do, qui pro pter nos ho mi
85
tr

89
E
nes et propter no - stram sa - lu - tem, qui pro - pter nos
93
ho - - mi - nes et propter nostram sa - lu - tem de - scen - dit de coe -

97
lis, de-scen - - - - - - - - - - - - - -
lis, de - scen - - dit, de - scen - - -
lis, de - scen - - - - - - - - - - - -
lis,descen - - - - - - - - - - - - -
lis,descen - - - - - - - - - - - - - -
97
102
- - - - - - - dit de coe - lis, de -
- - - - dit, de - scendit de coe - lis, de -
- - - - dit, de - scendit de coe - lis, de -
- - - - dit, de - scen - dit, de-scendit de coe - lis, de -
- - - - dit, de - scen - dit, de-scendit de coe - lis, de -
102

106
scen - dit de coelis, de coelis, de coe - - lis,
scen - dit de coelis, de coelis, de coe - - lis,
scen - dit de coelis, de coelis, de coe - - lis,
scen - dit de coelis, de coelis, de coe - - lis,
scen - dit de coelis, de coelis, de coe - - lis,
106
p
112
descen - - dit de coe - - lis.
de scen - - dit de coe - - lis.
descen - - dit de coe - - lis.
de - scen - - dit de coe - - lis.
de - scen - - dit de coe - - lis.
112
cresc.
f
3
3

10. Et Incarnatus Est

23
B
san - - cto, ex Ma_ri _ a vir_gi_ne et ho_mo fa_ctus
B
28
est, et ho _ mo fa -
32
- ctus est,
36
C
et ho _ mo fa _ ctus est, et
C
40
ho - - mo fa -

43
tr
D
ctus est.
D
47
dim.
Et in car na tus est
51
de spi ri tu san cto
55
ex Ma ri a vir gi ne et ho mo fa ctus est, et ho mo
E
E
60
tr
fa

64
ctus est,
fa
68
ctus est,
fa
72
F
ctus est,
fa
78
Cadenza
p
82

85
89
93
97
tr
ctus est.
p
102
calando

11. Crucifixus

6
dim.
— pro no - - bis, cru - ci - fi - - xus e - ti - am pro
dim.
cru - - ci - fi - - xus, cru - ci - fi - - xus
no - bis cru - ci - fi - - xus, cru - ci - fi - - xus
dim.
no - bis, cru - ci - fi - - xus, cruci - fi - xus e - - ti - am
dim.
6
dim.
8
A
mf
no - - bis, pro no - bis, sub Pon - ti - o Pi - la - to pas - sus
mf
e - ti - am pro no - bis, sub Pon - ti - o Pi - la - to pas - sus
mf
e - ti - am pro no - bis sub Pon - ti - o Pi - la - to pas - sus
mf
pro — no - bis sub Pon - ti - o Pi - la - to pas - sus
8
A
pp
mf
10
f
et se - pul - tus est, cruci - fi - - xus e - - ti - am sub
f
et se - pul - tus est, cru - - ci - fi - xus e - tiam sub
f
et se - pul - tus est, — cru - - ci - fi - xus e - ti - am sub
f
et se - pul - tus est, cru - - ci - fi - xus e - tiam sub
10
f

più Adagio
Pon - ti - o Pi - la - to pas - sus et se - pul - - -
Pon - ti - o Pi - la - to pas - sus et se -
Pon - ti - o Pi - la - to pas - sus et se -
Pon - ti - o Pi - la - to pas - sus et se -
più Adagio
- tus est, pas - sus, pas - - - sus et se - pul - tus est, pas -
pul - tus est, pas - sus, pas - - sus se - pul - tus est, pas -
pul - tus est, pas - sus et se - pul - tus est, pas -
pul - tus est, pas - sus et se - pul - tus est, pas -
più
più lento
morendo
- sus et sepul - tus est.
- sus et sepul - tus est.
- sus et sepul - tus est.
- sus et sepul - tus est.
lento
morendo
attacca

12. Et Resurrexit

7
ptu - ras, se - cun - dum scri - ptu - ras, se - cun - dum scri -
ptu - ras, se - cun - dum scri - ptu - ras, se - cun - dum scri -
ptu - ras, se - cun - dum scri - ptu - ras, se - cun - dum scri -
ptu - ras, se - cun - dum scri - ptu - ras, se - cun - dum scri -
7
9
A
p
ptu - ras. Et a -
ptu - ras. Et a-scen - dit
ptu - ras. Et a-scen - dit
ptu - ras. Et a-scen - dit
9
A
p
11
cresc
scen-dit, et a - scen - dit in coe - lum, a -
in coe - lum, a - scen-dit in coe-lum,
in coe - lum, a - scen-dit in coe-lum,
in coe - lum, a - scen-dit in coe-lum,
11
cresc

13
scen - dit a - scen - dit in coe - lum, se - dit ad
a - scen - dit in coe - lum,
a - scen - dit in coe - lum,
a - scen - dit in coe - lum,
13
15
dex - te - ram pa - tris, ad
se - det ad dex - te - ram pa - tris, ad
se - det ad dex - te - ram pa - tris, ad
se - det ad dex - te - ram pa - tris, ad
15
17
dex - te - ram pa - tris,
dex - te - ram pa - tris,
dex - te - ram pa - tris,
dex - te - ram pa - tris,
17

19
B
et i - te - rum ven -
et i - te -
19
B
21
tu - - - - rus
est cum glo - ri - a, et i - te -
rum ven - - tu - - rus
est cum glo - ri - a,
et i - te - rum ven -
21
23
rum ven - - tu - - - rus
est cum glo - ri - a,
et
et i - te - rum ven -
tu - - - - rus est cum glo - ri - a, et i - te - rum ven -
23

25
i - te - rum ven - tu - rus est cum glo - ri - a,
tu - - - - rus est cum glo - - ri - a, et i - te -
tu - - - rus est cum glo - - ri - a, et
et i - te - rum ven -
27
et i - te - rum ven - tu - rus est cum glo - ri - a ju - di - ca - - -
rum ven - tu - - - rus est cum glo - ri - a ju - di -
i - te - rum ven - tu - - rus est cum glo - ri - a
tu - - - - - rus est cum glo - - ri - a ju - di - ca - re,
29
- - - - - re vi - vos et mor - tu - os, et
ca - - - - re vi - vos et mor - tu - os, et
ju - di - ca - re vi - vos, vi - vos et mor - tu - os, et
ju - - di - ca - re vi - vos et mor - tu - os, et
p

31
C
mor - - - - - tu - os, et i - te - rum
mor - - tu - - - os, ven -
mor - - - tu - - - os, ven -
mor - - - - tu - os, ven -
cresc
33
ven - tu - rus est cum glo - - - - - ri - a, cu - jus
tu - - rus est cum glo - - ri - a cu - jus
tu - - rus est cum glo - - ri - a cu - jus
tu - - rus est cum glo - - ri - - a cu - jus
tr
35
re - gni non e - rit fi - - - - - nis, cu - jus
re - gni non e - rit fi - - - - - nis, cu - jus
re - gni non e - rit fi - - - - - nis, cu - jus
re - gni non e - rit fi - - - - - nis, cu - jus

37
re - gni non e - rit fi - nis, cu - jus re - gni non
re - gni non e - rit fi - nis, cu - jus re - gni non
re - gni non e - rit fi - nis, cu - jus re - gni non
re - gni non e - rit fi - nis, cu - jus re - gni non
37
39
D
p
e - rit fi - nis, cu - jus
e - rit fi - nis, non, non e - rit
e - rit fi - nis, non, non e - rit
e - rit fi - nis, non, non e - rit
39
D
p
41
cresc.
re - gni non e - rit fi - nis, cu - jus
fi - nis, non e - rit, non e - rit,
fi - nis, non e - rit, non e - rit,
fi - nis, non e - rit, non e - rit,
41
cresc.

43
re - - gni non e - rit fi - - - nis, non e - rit
non e - - - - rit fi - - nis,
non e - - - - rit fi - - nis,
non e - - - - rit fi - - nis,
43
45
fi - - - - - - - - - - - nis,
non e - rit fi - - - - - - - - nis,
non e - rit fi - - - - - - - - nis,
non e - rit fi - - - - - - - - nis,
45
47
non e - rit fi - - nis, cu - jus
non e - rit fi - - nis, cu - jus
non e - rit fi - - nis, cu - jus
non e - rit fi - - nis, cu - jus
47

13. Et in Spiritum Sanctum

12
18
24
SOLO A Tenor
Et in Spi - ritum sanctum,
tr
A
mf
29
Do - minum, et vi - vi - fi - can-tem,
p
f
34 Soprano TUTTI
Et in Spi - ri-tum san - ctum, Do - mi - num, et in
Alto TUTTI
Et in Spi - ri-tum san - ctum, Do - mi - num,
Tenor TUTTI
Et in Spi - ri-tum san - ctum, Do - mi - num, Do - minum,
Bass TUTTI
Et in Spi - ri-tum san - ctum, Do - mi - num, et in
34

39
Do - mi - num vi - vi - fi - can - tem,
et vi - vi - fi - can - tem,
SOLO
et vi - vi - fi - can - tem, qui ex Pa - tre
Do - mi - num vi - vi - fi - can - tem,
39
p
44
Fi - li - o - que, Fi - li - o - que pro - ce - dit,
44
49
qui ex Pa - tre Fi - li - o - que pro - ce - dit,
TUTTI
qui ex
49
f

54
B
TUTTI
qui ex Pa - tre Fi - li - o - que
TUTTI
qui ex Pa - tre Fi - li - o - que
TUTTI
qui ex Pa - tre Fi - li - o - que
Pa - - tre Fi-li - o - - - - - - - - que
54
B
f
59
pro - ce - - - dit;
pro - ce - - - dit;
tr
pro - ce - - - dit;
pro - ce - - - dit;
59
tr
64
SOLO
qui cum Pa - tre
64
tr
p

69
et Fi - li-o si - mul ad-o - ra - tur, et con - glori-fi-
69
74
C TUTTI
qui cum Pa - tre, cum Pa - tre et fi - li - o
TUTTI
qui cum Pa - tre, cum Pa - tre et fi - li - o
ca - tur;
TUTTI
qui cum Pa - tre, cum Pa - tre et fi - lí - o
TUTTI
qui cum Pa - tre, cum Pa - tre et fi - li - o
74
C
79
si - mul, si - mul ad - o - ra - tur,
si - mul, si - mul ad - o - ra - tur,
si - mul, si - mul ad - o - ra - tur,
si - mul, si - mul ad - o - ra - tur,
79

84
TUTTI
qui lo -
TUTTI
qui lo -
SOLO
qui lo - cu - - tus est per pro - phe - tas,
TUTTI
qui lo - cu - -
84
90
cu - tus, qui lo - cu - tus est, qui lo - cu - tus est per pro -
cu - tus, qui lo - cu - tus est, qui lo - cu - tus est per pro -
TUTTI
qui lo - cu - tus, qui lo - cu - tus est per pro -
- tus est per pro - phe - - tas, qui lo - cu - tus est per pro -
90
96
phe - - tas,
phe - - tas,
SOLO
phe - - tas, qui lo - cu - tus est per pro - phe - tas,
phe - - tas,
96

102 D
TUTTI
qui lo - cu - tus est per pro - phe - - - tas,
TUTTI
qui lo - cu - tus est per pro - phe - - - tas,
TUTTI
qui lo - cu - tus est per pro - phe - - - tas,
TUTTI
qui lo - cu - tus est per pro - phe - - - tas,
102 D
108
per pro - phe - - - tas.
per pro - phe - - - tas.
per pro - phe - - - tas.
per pro - phe - - - tas.
108
114
119
rit.
attacca

14. Credo in Unam Sanctam

10
sto - li-cam ec - - cle-siam, con - fi-te-or, con -
sto - li-cam ec - - cle-siam, con - fi-te-or, con -
sto - li-cam ec - - cle-siam, con - fi-te-or, con -
sto - li-cam ec - - cle-siam, con - fi-te-or, con -
13
A
fi - te-or u - - num ba - ptis - - - -
fi - te-or u - - num ba - ptis - - - -
fi - te-or u - - num ba - ptis - ma, ba -
fi - te-or u - - num ba - ptis - - ma, ba -
16
- - - ma in re - missio-nem pec - - ca - to - - rum,
- ma in remissi-o-nem pec - - ca - to - - rum, in
ptis - ma re - mis - sio-nem pec - ca - to - - rum,
ptis - ma in re - mis - sio-nem pec - - ca - to - - rum,

20
p
et ex - pe-cto, ex - pe - - cto
dim.
re-missio - nem pec - cato - - rum,
dim.
in re - mis - sionem peccato - - rum,
20
tr
dim
p
24
cresc.
re - sur - re - ctionem,
cresc.
p
re - - sur - re - ctionem, et ex - pe-cto, ex - pe - cto
cresc.
re - - sur - re - ctionem,
cresc.
re - - sur - re - ctionem,
24
cresc.
f
p
28
cresc.
p
re - - sur - re - ctio-nem mor - tu -
cresc.
p
re - - sur - re - ctio-nem mor - tu -
cresc.
p
re - - sur - re - ctio-nem mor - tu -
cresc.
p
re - - sur - re - ctio-nem mor - - tu -
28
cresc.
f
p

31
B
o - rum,
mor - tu - o -
o - rum,
mortu - o -
o - rum,
mortu - o -
o - rum,
mortu - o -
31
B
34
rum.
Cre - do,
rum.
Cre - do,
rum.
Cre - do,
rum.
Cre - do,
34
cresc.
37
Cre - do
in u - nam
Cre - do
Cre - do
Cre - do
37
3

40
san - ctam ca - tho - li-cam et a - posto - li -
in u - nam san - ctam et a - posto - li -
in u - nam san - ctam ca-tho - li -
in u - nam ca-tho - li -
40
43
cam, et a - po - sto - li-cam ec - cle-siam, con -
cam, et a - po - sto - li-cam ec - cle-siam, con -
cam, et a - po - sto - li-cam ec - cle-siam, con -
cam, et a - po - sto - li-cam ec - cle-siam, con -
43
46
fi - te-or, con - fi - te-or u - num ba -
fi - te-or, con - fi - te-or u - num ba -
fi - te-or, con - fi - te-or u - num ba -
fi - te-or, con - fi - te-or u - num ba -
46
C

49
ptis - - ma in re - mis - sio - nem pec - ca - to - - -
ptis - - - - - - - - ma in re - mis - sio - nem pec - ca -
ptis - ma, ba - ptis - ma in re - mis - sio - nem pec - ca -
ptis - - - - - - ma in re - mis - - sio - nem pec - ca -
49
52
- - - - - - - - - rum, in re - mis -
to - - - - - - - - - rum, in re - mis - sio - nem, re - mis -
to - - - - - - - - - rum, in re - mis - sio - nem
to - - - - - - - - - rum, in re - mis -
52
55
sionem pecca - to - - rum, et ex - pe - - - - - -
sionem pecca to - - - rum, et ex - pe - cto
pec - ca - to - - - - rum, et ex -
sionem pecca - to - - - rum, ex - - pe - - - - - -
55

58
cto re - sur - re - ctio - - nem mor - - - tu - - -
re - sur - re - ctio - - nem mor - - tu - - -
pe - - - cto re - sur - re - ctio - - - nem
cto re - sur-re - ctio - - - - - - nem
58
61
o - - - - - - - rum, mor - tu - - o - - rum,
o - - rum, mor - - tu - o - rum,
mor - - tu - o - - - - - - - rum,
mor - - - - tu - - o - - - - - - - - - rum,
61
64
pp
mor - tu - o - rum.
pp
mor - tu - o - rum.
pp
mor - tu - o - rum.
pp
mor - tu - o - rum.
64
Ob.
Fag.
attacca

15. Et Vitam Venturi

19
A
sae - culi, a - - - - - - men, a - - men,
ven - tu - ri sae - cu - li, a - men, a - men, a - - -
a - - - - men, et vi - tam ven - tu - ri
et vi - tam ventu - ri sae - culi, a -
25
a - - - - - - - - - men, et
- - - - - - - - - - - - - - - men,
sae - culi, et vi - tam
- - - - - - - - - - - - - - men, a - men,
30
vi - tam ven - tu - ri sae - cu - li, a - men, a - men,
et vi - tam ventu - ri
ventu - ri sae - culi, a - - - - - - - men, et vi - tam
a - men, a - - - - - men, a -

36
et vi - tam ven - tu - ri
sae - culi, a - - - - - - - men, a -
ven - tu - ri sae - cu - li, et vi - tam
- - men, a - men, a - men,
36
41
sae - culi, et vi - tam ven - tu - ri sae - culi,
- men, a - men, a - men, a - - - - - - men,
ven - tu - ri sae - cu - li, a - - - men, a - men,
et vi - tam ventu - ri sae - cu - li, a - - - men,
41
47 B
a - men, a - men, a - men, a - men, a - - - - -
a - - - men, a - - - men, a -
a - men, a - men, a - men, a - men, a - - - -
a - - - men, a - - - - - - - -
47 B

52
- men, a -
- men, a -
- men, a -
- men, a -
52
58
men, et vi - tam, et vi - tam,
men, a - - - - - - - - men, et vi - tam, et
men, a - - - - - - - - men, a - men, a - men,
men, et vi - tam,
58
65 C
et vi - tam, et vi - tam ventu - ri
vi - tam, et vi - tam, ven - tu - ri sae - cu - li a -
a - men, a - men, a - men, a - men,
et vi - tam, et vi - tam, et vi - tam
65 C

72
sae - culi, a - - - - - - - - - - - - - men, a - men,
- men, a - men, a - - - - - men, et
et vi - tam
ven - tu - ri sae - cu - li, a - - - - - - - men,
72
78
a - men, a - men, et vi - tam ven -
vi - tam ven - tu - ri sae - cu - li, et vi - tam ven - tu - ri
ventu - ri sae - culi, a - - - - - men, et
et vi - tam, ven - tu - ri sae - cu - li, a - men,
78
84
D
tu - ri sae - cu - li, a - - - - - - - - - - men, a - men,
sae - culi, a - - - - - men, a - - - - - - men, et
vi - tam ven - tu - ri sae - culi, a - - - - - - - men
a - - - men, et vi - tam,
84
D

90
a - men,
a - men,
a - - men, a - men,
vi - tam,
et
vi - tam,
et
vi - tam
ven - tu - ri
sae - culi,
a - men,
a - men,
a - men,
a - men,
et
vi - tam,
et
vi - tam,
ven - tu - ri
sae - culi,
et
90
97
a - men,
a - men,
a - men, a - - men,
et
vi - tam
ven - tu - ri
sae - culi,
et
vi - tam ven -
a - men,
a - - men, a - men, a - men,
a - - men,
vi - tam
ven - tu - ri
sae - cu - li,
et
vi - tam ven - tu - ri, ven -
97
103
E
amen, a - - men,
et
vi - tam
ven -
tu - ri sae - cu - li,
et
vi - tam
ven - tu - ri sae - cu -
a - - men,
et
vi - tam
ventu - ri
sae - culi,
tu - ri sae - cu - li,
et
vi - tam
ventu - ri
sae - culi,
a - men,
103
E

110
tu-ri sae-cu-li, a - - - - - - - - - - - - men, a -
li, a - men, a - men, a - - - - - - - - - - - - - men, a -
a - - - men, a - - - - - - - - - - - men, a -
a - - - - - - - men, a - men, a - - - - - - - - - men, a -
110
116
men, a - - - - - - - - men, a - - - - - - - men,
men, a - - - - - - - - men, a - - - - - - - men,
men, a - - - - - men, a - - men, a - - - men, a - men,
men, a - - - - - - - - men, a - - - - - - - men,
116
tr
121
a - - - - - - men, a - - men.
a - - - - men, a - - men.
a - - men, a - men, a - - men.
a - - - - men, a - - men.
rit.
121

16. Sanctus

Largo
Soprano
Alto
Tenor
Bass
Soprano
Alto
Tenor
Bass
Piano
San - ctus, San - ctus, San - ctus
ff
p
Do - - - - mi-nus Deus Sa - baoth,
Do - - - - mi-nus Deus

Do - - - - - mi-nus De-us Sa - baoth, Do-mi-nus De-us
Do - - - - - mi-nus De-us Sa - baoth, Do-mi-nus De-us
Do - - - - - mi-nus De-us Sa - baoth, Do-mi-nus De-us
Do - - - - - mi-nus De-us Sa - baoth, Do-mi-nus De-us
Sa - baoth, Do - - mi-nus, Do-mi-nus De-us
Sa - baoth, Do - - mi-nus, Do-mi-nus De-us
Sa - baoth, Do - - mi-nus, Do-mi-nus De-us
Sa - baoth, Do - - mi-nus, Do-mi-nus De-us
cresc.
A
Sa - baoth, ple - ni sunt coe - li et ter - ra,
Sa - baoth, ple - ni sunt coe - li et ter - ra,
Sa - baoth, ple - ni sunt coe - li et ter - ra,
Sa - baoth, ple - ni sunt coe - li et ter - ra,
Sa - baoth, ple - ni, ple - ni
Sa - baoth, ple - ni, ple - ni
Sa - baoth, ple - ni, ple - ni
Sa - baoth, ple - ni, ple - ni

13
ple-ni sunt coe-li et ter - ra
ple-ni sunt coe-li et ter - ra
ple-ni sunt coe-li et ter - ra
ple-ni sunt coe-li et ter - ra
13
sunt coe-li et ter-ra, sunt coe-li et ter - ra
sunt coe-li et ter-ra, sunt coe-li et ter - ra
sunt coe-li et ter-ra, sunt coe-li et ter - ra
sunt coe-li et ter-ra, sunt coe-li et ter - ra
13
15
glo-ri-a, glo-ri-a tu - a.
glo-ri-a tu - a.
glo-ri-a, glo-ri-a tu - a.
glo-ri-a tu - a.
15
glo-ri-a, glo-ri-a tu - a.
glo-ri-a tu - a.
glo-ri-a tu - a.
glo-ri-a tu - a.
15
attacca

17. Osanna I

18 Allegro comodo
in ex - cel - - - - - - - -
O - san - na in ex - cel - sis, o - - san - - - - - - - - -
O - san - na in ex - cel - sis, o - - san - - - - - - - - -
18 Allegro comodo
20
in ex -
- - - - - - - - - - - sis, in ex - cel - sis, o -
- - - - - - na in ex - cel - - - - sis, o - san - na,
O - san - na in ex - cel - sis, o -
- - - - - - na in ex - cel - - - - sis, o -

22
cel - - - - - - - - - - - - -
san - - - - - - na in ex - cel - - sis, in ex -
o - san - na, o - san - na in ex - cel - - -
22
f
O -
san - - - - - - - - - - - na, o -
san - na, o - san - na, o - san - na in ex - cel - - -
22
24
f
B
in ex - cel - - - - - - - -
sis, in ex - cel - sis, o - - san - - - - - - na
cel - - - - - - - - sis, o - san - na, o -
- - - - sis, o - san - na, o - san - na, o - san - na
24
san - na in ex - cel - sis, o - - san - - - - - - -
san - - - - - na, o - san - na, o - san - na
- - - - sis, o - san - na, o - san - na, o -
24
B

26
- - - - - - - - sis, in ex-celsis, o- - san-na, o-san-na, o-
in ex-cel - - - - - - - - - sis, o- - san-na, o - san-na, o-
san-na, o-san-na in ex-cel - sis o - san-na, o-san-na, o-
in ex-cel - - sis, in ex-cel - - - - - - -
26
O - san-na in ex-celsis, o- - san - - - - - -
- - na, o - san - - - na, o-san-na, o-san-na,
in ex-cel - - - - - - - - sis, o-san-na, o-san-na,
san - na in ex-cel - - sis, in ex-cel - - - - - -
26
29
san - - na in ex - cel-sis, in ex - cel - - sis,
san - - na, o-san - na, o-sanna in ex-
san - - na in ex-cel-sis, in ex-cel -
- - - - sis, o-san-na, o-san-na, o-sanna, o-san -
29
- - na in ex - cel-sis, in ex - cel - - sis,
o - san - na, o-sanna in ex-
o - san - na, o-sanna, o-sanna, o-san-na,
- - - sis, in ex-cel-sis, in ex-celsis, o -
29

32
celsis, o - san - - - - - - - - - - na, o -
- sis, o - san - - - - na in ex - cel - sis, in ex - cel - sis, in ex -
na, o - sanna, o - san - na in ex - cel - - - - - -
32
in ex - cel - - - - - - - - - - - - sis,
celsis, o - san - - - - - - - - na, o - san - na in ex -
o - san - - na
sanna, o - sanna, o - san - na, o - san - na in ex - cel - - - - - -
32
35
in ex cel - - - - - - - sis,
C
sanna, o - san - - - - - - - na, o - san - - - - - -
celsis, o - san - na, o - sanna,
- sis, o - san - na, o - san - na, o - san - na in ex - cel - sis, o - san - na, o -
35
in ex - cel - - - - - - -
celsis, o - san - - - - - - - na, o - san - - - - - -
in ex - cel - sis, o - sanna, o - sanna, o - sanna, o - san - na,
sis, o - san - na, o - sanna in ex - cel - sis, o - san - na, o -
35
C
Z269991

38
na, o-san-na, o-san-na, o-san-na in ex-
o-san-na in ex-ce-sis, o san-
san-na in ex-cel- sis, o
sis, o-san-na, o-sanna, o-sanna, o-san-
na
o-san-na, o-san-na, o-sanna in ex-cel-sis,
sanna in ex-cel- sis, o-
41
o-sanna in ex-cel-sis, o-san-
cel- sis, o-sanna, o-sanna in ex-
na in ex-cel-sis, o-sanna, o-sanna, o-san-
san-na in ex-cel- sis o-
na in ex-cel- sis, o-san- na in ex-
in ex-cel-
o-sanna in ex-cel-sis, o-sanna, o-san-
san-na in ex-cel- sis, o-sanna, o-san-na, o-san-na, o-

44
na, o - san - - na, o - sanna, o - sanna in ex - cel - - - -
cel - - - sis, o - sanna, o - sanna in — ex - cel - - -
na, o - sanna, o - san - - - - - - - na in ex - cel -
sanna in ex - cel - sis, o - san - - - - - - - na in ex - cel -
44
cel - sis, o - san - na in ex - cel - - - - - - - - - - - -
- - - - sis, o - san - na, o - san - na, o - san - na in ex - cel - - -
na in ex - cel - sis, o - san - - - - - - - na in ex - cel -
sanna in ex - cel - sis, o - san - - - - - - - na in ex - cel -
44
47
sis, o - san - - - - - - - - - - - - na,
sis, o - san - - na, o - sanna in ex -
sis, o - san - - - - - na,
sis, o - - - san - na in ex - cel - sis, o -
47
sis, o - san - - - - - - - - - - - - na,
sis, o - san - - - na, o - sanna in ex -
sis, o - san - - - - - na,
sis, o - - - san - na in ex - cel - sis, o -
47

50
D
o - - - san - na in ex - cel-sis, in ex - cel - - - - - -
cel-sis, o - san - - - - - - - - - - na, o-san-na, o-san-na,
o - - - san - na in ex - cel-sis, o-san-na, o-san-na,
san-na in ex-cel-sis, o - - san - - - - - - - - na, o-san-na, o-san-na,
50
o - - - san - na in ex - cel-sis, in ex - cel - - - - - -
cel-sis, o - san - - - - - - - - - - na, o-san-na, o-san-na
o - - - san - na in ex - cel-sis, o-san-na, o-san-na
san-na in ex-cel-sis, o - - san - - - - - - - - na, o-san-na, o-san-na
50
D
53
- - sis, o - san - - - - - - - - - - - - na
o - san - - - - - - - - - - - na
o - san - - - - - - - - - - na
o - san - - - - - - - - - - - na
53
- - - sis, o - - - san - na in ex - cel - sis,
in ex-cel - sis, o - - - san - na in ex - cel - sis,
in ex-cel - sis, o - - - san - na in ex - cel - sis,
in ex-cel - sis, o - - - san - na in ex - cel - sis,
53

56
in ex_cel_sis, o_san_na in ex_cel_sis, in ex_cel_sis,
in ex_cel_sis, o_san_na in ex_cel_sis, in ex_cel_sis,
in ex_cel_sis, o_san_na in ex_cel_sis, in ex_cel_sis,
in ex_cel_sis, o_san_na in ex_cel_sis, in ex_cel_sis,
56
in ex_cel_sis, o_san_na in ex_cel_sis, o_
in ex_cel_sis, o_san_na in ex_cel_sis, o_
in ex_cel_sis, o_san_na in ex_cel_sis, o_
in ex_cel_sis, o_san_na in ex_cel_sis, o_
56
59
o_san_na in ex_cel_sis, in excel_sis, in excel_sis.
o_san_na in ex_cel_sis, in excel_sis, in excel_sis.
o_san_na in ex_cel_sis, in excel_sis, in excel_sis.
o_san_na in ex_cel_sis, in excel_sis, in excel_sis.
59
san_na in ex_cel_sis, in ex_cel_sis, in excel_sis, in excel_sis.
san_na in ex_cel_sis, in ex_cel_sis, in excel_sis, in excel_sis.
san_na in ex_cel_sis, in ex_cel_sis, in excel_sis, in excel_sis.
san_na in ex_cel_sis, in ex_cel_sis, in excel_sis, in excel_sis.
59

18. Benedictus

17
be - ne - di - ctus qui ve - nit in no - mine do - mi - ni,
be - ne - di - ctus qui ve - nit in no - mine do - mi - ni,
Be - ne - di - ctus qui ve - nit in no - mine do - mi - ni,
Be - ne - di - ctus qui ve - nit in no - mine do - mi - ni,
17
f
21
be - ne - di - ctus qui ve - nit, be - ne -
be - ne - di - ctus qui ve - nit, be - ne - di -
21
p
24
be - ne - di - ctus qui ve - nit, qui
be - ne - di - ctus qui venit, bene - di - ctus qui ve - nit, qui
di - ctus qui ve -
- ctus qui ve - nit, qui
24

27
ve - - - - - - - - - - - - - - - -
ve - - - - - - - - - - - - nit, qui
- nit, be - ne - di - ctus qui ve - - nit, qui ve - nit, qui
ve - nit, be - ne - di - ctus qui ve - - - - - -
27
30
- - - - - - - nit, qui ve - - - - - - - -
ve - - - - - nit, qui ve - - - - - - - -
ve - nit, qui ve - - - - - - - - - - -
nit, qui ve - - - - - - -
30
33
B
- nit, qui ve - nit in no - mi - ne, in
- nit, qui ve - nit in no - mine, in
- nit, qui ve - nit in no - mine, in
- nit in
33
B

36
no - mine do - - mi - ni, be - ne - di - ctus, be - ne -
no - mi - ne do - - mi - ni, be - ne - di - ctus, be - ne -
no - mi - ne do - - mi - ni, be - ne - di - ctus, be - ne -
no - mine do - - mi - ni, be - ne - di - - ctus, be - ne - di - - -
39
di - ctus qui ve - - nit in
di - ctus qui ve - - - - - nit in
di - ctus qui ve - - - - - - - nit in
ctus qui ve - - - - - - - - - - nit in
42
no - mine do - - mi - ni, in no - - - - mi - ne do - mi - ni, in no - - -
no - mine do - - mi - ni, in no - - - mi - ne do - mi - ni, in no - - -
no - mine do - - mi - ni, in no - - - - mi - ne do - mi - ni, in no - - -
no - mine do - - mi - ni, in no - - - - mi - ne do - mi - ni, in no - - -

46
- mi-ne do- - mi-ni!
- mi-ne do- - mi-ni!
- mi-ne do- - mi-ni!
- mi-ne do- - mi-ni!
46
f
49
49
tr
52
C p
Be - ne - di - - - - ctus qui ve - nit in no-mi - ne do-mini,
p
Be - ne - di - - - - ctus qui ve-nit in no-mi - ne do- mini,
p
Be - ne - - di - - - ctus qui ve - nit, qui ve-nit,
p
Be - ne- - di - - ctus qui ve-nit
52
C
p
f

55
be - ne - di - - - - ctus qui ve - nit in no-mi - - ne
be - ne - di - - - - ctus qui ve-nit in no-mi - - ne
be - ne - di - ctus qui ve - nit in no - mi - ne
be - ne - di - - - ctus qui
55
p
58
do - mini, qui ve - - - nit, qui
do - mini, qui ve - - - nit,
do - mini, qui ve - - - nit qui
ve - nit, qui ve -
58
f
p
61
ve - nit in no - mi-ne do - mi-ni, qui ve - - - - nit, qui
qui ve-nit in no-mine do - mi-ni, qui ve - - - nit, qui
ve-nit in no - mi-ne do - mi-ni, qui ve - - - nit, qui ve -
- nit in no-mine do - mi-ni, qui ve - - - nit, qui
61
cresc.

64
ve - nit,
ve - nit,
nit, be - ne - di - ctus qui ve - nit,
ve - nit.
67
D
be - ne - di -
be - ne - di -
be - ne -
be - ne - di - ctus qui ve - nit, be - ne -
70
ctus qui ve - nit in nomi - ne do - mi - ni, be - ne - di - ctus qui
ctus qui ve - nit in nomi - ne do - mi - ni,
di - ctus qui venit in nomi - ne do - mi - ni,
di - ctus qui venit in nomi - ne do - mi - ni,

74
ve-nit, be-ne-di - - - ctus, be - - - -
be - ne - di - ctus qui ve-nit, be-ne - di - ctus,
be - ne-di - ctus qui
74
77
- ne - di - - ctus qui ve - - - nit, qui
be - - - - ne - - di - - ctus qui
ve-nit, be-ne-di - - - - - ctus qui
be - ne - di - ctus qui ve-nit, be-ne - di - - - ctus qui
77
80
ve - - - nit, qui ve - - - nit, qui ve - -
ve - - nit, qui ve - - -
ve - - nit,
ve - - nit, qui
80

83
E
nit, qui ve - - - - nit, qui
- nit, qui ve - - - - - - nit, qui
qui ve - - - - - - - - - - nit, qui
ve - - - - - - - - - - - - - nit,
83
E
cresc
p
86
ve - nit in no - mi - ne, in no - mine do - - mi -
ve - nit in no - mine, in no - mine do - - mi -
ve - nit in no - mine, in no - mine do - - mi -
in no - mine do - - mi -
86
cresc
89
ni, be - ne - di - ctus, be - ne - di - ctus
ni, be - ne - di - ctus, be - ne - di - ctus
ni, qui ve - nit, qui ve - nit, qui
ni, be - ne - di - - ctus, be - ne - di - - ctus qui ve - - -
89
p

92
qui ve - nit, qui ve - - nit in
qui ve - - - - - - - nit in
ve - - - - - - - - - nit in
- - - - - - - - - - - nit in
92
95
no - mi - ne do - mi - ni, in no - - - mi - ne do - mi -
no - mi - ne - do - mi - ni, in no - - - mi - ne do - mi -
no - mi - ne do - mi - ni, in no - - - mi - ne do - mi -
no - mi - ne do - mi - ni, in no - - - mi - ne do - mi -
95
98
cresc.
rit.
ni, in no - - mi - ne, in no - - mine do - mi -
ni, in no - - mi - ne, in no - - mine do - mi -
ni, in no - - mi - ne, in no - - mine do - mi -
ni, in no - - mi - ne, in no - - mine do - mi -
98
cresc
rit.

[Osanna II]

102
F a tempo
nı!
ni!
ni!
ni!
F a tempo
(104)
tr
107
O - san - - na,
O - san - - na, o - sanna in ex -
O - san - - na,
O - - san - na in ex - cel - sis, o -
107
O - san - - na,
O - san - - na, o - sanna in ex -
O - san - - na,
O - - san - na in ex - cel - sis, o -
107

110
o - - - san - na in ex - cel - sis, in ex - cel - - - - - - -
celsis, o - san - - - - - - - - - - na, o - san - na, o - san - na,
o - - - san - na in ex - cel - sis, o - san - na, o - san - na,
sanna in ex - celsis, o - - san - - - - - - - na, o - san - na, o - san - na,
110
o - - - san - na in ex - cel - sis, in ex - cel - - - - - - -
celsis, o - san - - - - - - - - - - na, o - san - na, o - san - na
o - - - san - na in ex - cel - sis, o - san - na, o - san - na
sanna in ex - celsis, o - - san - - - - - - - na, o - san - na, o - san - na
110
113
- - - sis, o - san - - - - - - - - - - - na
o - - san - - - - - - - - - - na
o - - san - - - - - - - - - - - na
o - - san - - - - - - - - - - - na
113
- - - - sis, o - - - san - na in ex - cel - sis,
in ex - cel - - sis, o - - - san - na in ex - cel - sis,
in ex - cel - - sis, o - - - san - na in ex - cel - sis,
in ex - cel - - sis, o - - - san - na in ex - cel - sis,
113

116
in ex - cel - sis, o - san - na in ex - cel - sis, in ex - cel - sis,
in ex - cel - sis, o - san - na in ex - cel - sis, in ex - cel - sis,
in ex - cel - sis, o - san - na in ex - cel - sis, in ex - cel - sis,
in ex - cel - sis, o - san - na in ex - cel - sis, in ex - cel - sis,
116
in ex - cel - sis, o - san - na in ex - cel - sis, o -
in ex - cel - sis, o - san - na in ex - cel - sis, o -
in ex - cel - sis, o - san - na in ex - cel - sis, o -
in ex - cel - sis, o - san - na in ex - cel - sis, o -
116
119
o - san - na in ex - cel - sis, in excel - sis, in excel - sis.
o - san - na in ex - cel - sis, in excel - sis, in excel - sis.
o - san - na in ex - cel - sis, in excel - sis, in excel - sis.
o - san - na in ex - cel - sis, in excel - sis, in excel - sis.
119
san - na in ex - cel - sis, in ex - cel - sis, in excel - sis, in excel - sis.
san - na in ex - cel - sis, in ex - cel - sis, in excel - sis, in excel - sis.
san - na in ex - cel - sis, in ex - cel - sis, in excel - sis, in excel - sis.
san - na in ex - cel - sis, in ex - cel - sis, in excel - sis, in excel - sis.
119

19. Agnus Dei

Andante moderato
Piano
p
TUTTI
A - gnus De - i qui
A - gnus
tol - lis pec - ca - ta mun - di, mi - se - re - re
De - i qui tol - lis pec - ca - ta mun - di,
A - gnus De - i, agnus De - i,
A - gnus, agnus De - i,
f

11
no - - bis, no - - - - - - - - bis, a - gnus De - i qui
mi - -
11
14
tol - lis pecca - ta, qui tol - lis pecca - ta, qui tol_lis pec_ca_ta
- - se - re - re no - - bis, no - - - - - - -
14
17
A
mun_di, mi_se_re - - re, qui tol - - lis, qui
bis, mi - se_re - - re, a_gnus De - i
mi - - - se - re - re
a - gnus De - i qui tol - lis pec_ca - ta, pec_
17
A

tol - - lis pec - ca - - - - - - ta, pec-ca - - -
mi - se-re - re no - bis, mi - - se-re-re
no - - bis, no - - - - - - - - bis, qui tol-lis pecca - - ta mun-di, qui tol-lis pec-ca-ta, qui tol-lis pec-ca-ta,
- - ta mun - - di, mi - se - re - re
no - - - - - - - - bis, mi - se - re - - re
ca - ta, pec - ca - ta mun - - di, mi - se - -
qui tol-lis pec - ca - ta, mi - - - se - re - -
no - - - - - - - bis,
no - - - - - - - bis,
re - - re no - - - - bis,
- - re no - - - - - bis,

27
p
a - gnus De - i qui tol - lis pec - ca - ta, pec - ca - ta
a - gnus De - - - i, a - - - gnus
a - gnus De - - - - i, a - - - gnus
a - gnus De - - - i, a - - - -
30
mun - di, mi - se - re - re no - - - bis,
De - - - - - - - - - - - i,
De - - - - - - - - - - - i,
- - gnus De - - - - - - i,
33
SOLO Soprano
B
do - - - na no - bis, do - na no - - - bis
tr

37
pa - cem, do - - - na, do - na no - bis pa - - -
p TUTTI
do - na nobis pa - cem,
p TUTTI
do - na nobis pa - cem,
p TUTTI
do - na no - bis pa - cem,
p TUTTI
do - na no - bis pa - cem,
37
p
42
cem, a - - - - - - gnus De - i qui
cresc.
p
do - - - na pa - cem, agnus De - i
p
do - - - na pa - cem, agnus De - i
p
do - - - na pa - cem, agnus De - i
p
do - - - na pa - cem, agnus De - i
42
p

47
f
p
tol - lis pec - ca - ta mun - di, mi - se - re - - re no - bis,
cresc.
qui tol - lis pec - ca - ta mun - di,
cresc.
qui tol - lis pec - ca - ta mun - di,
cresc.
qui tol - lis pec - ca - ta mun - di,
cresc.
qui tol - lis pec - ca - ta mun - di,
47
cresc.
51
do - - na no - bis pa - cem, do - na no - bis
pp
57
pa - - cem, do - na no - bis, do - na no - bis, do - na

61
C
tr
no - bis pa_cem, do_na
TUTTI p
do_na no_bis, do_na pa_cem.
TUTTI p
do - - - - - na pa_cem.
TUTTI p
pa- - - - - - cem.
TUTTI p
pa- - - - - - cem.
61
C
65
tr
tr
pa - - - - - - - - - - - - - - - - -
68
tr
- - - - - - - - - - - - - cem.
TUTTI
f
A -
68
f

72
-gnus De-i, a - - - - - - - gnus De-i qui
72
75
tol - lis pec - ca - - - - ta mun-di, pec -
TUTTI f
qui tol - lis pec-ca - ta mi-se-re-re,
TUTTI f
A - - - - gnus De - i, a-gnus De -
TUTTI f
A - gnus De-i qui
75
78
ca - - ta mun - di mi - - se - - re - re
mi - se - re - re, mi - se - re - re
- - i mi - se - - re - - re, mi - se -
tol - lis pec - ca - ta, pec - ca - - ta mun - di,
78
tr
tr
tr
tr

80
no - - - - - - - - bis, qui tol - - - - - lis pec_ca - - -
no _ bis, mi - se_re_re no - - bis, mi_se_
re - - - - - - - re, qui tol_lis pec_ca_ta, qui tol_lis pec_
qui tol_lis pec_ca_ta, qui tol_lis pec_ca_ta, qui tol_lis pec_ca_ta,
80
83
- - _ta mun_di, mi - se - re - - - re no - - - - -
re - - - re, mi - se - re - - - re no - - - - -
ca - ta, pec_ca - - ta, mi - se - re - - - re no - -
pec - ca_ta mun_di, mi - se_re - - - re no - - - - -
83
85
D
p
bis, do - na no - bis, do_na no_bis
bis, do - - na pa - - cem, do_na
bis, do - - na pa - - cem, do_na
bis, do - - na pa - - cem,
85
D
p

88
pa - cem, do - na nobis pa - cem, do - na no - bis pa -
no - bis pa - cem, do - na no - bis pa -
no - bis pa - cem, do - na no - bis pa -
no - bis pa - cem, do - na no - bis pa -
91
cem, do - na pa - cem, do - na no-bis,
cem, do - na pa - cem, do - na,
cem, do - na pa - cem,
cem, do - na pa - cem,
pp
p
94
do - na no-bis pa - cem.
do - na no-bis pa - cem.
do - na no-bis pa - cem.
do - na pa - cem.
dim.
pp
Ped.
Fine

SERENISSIMA MUSIC, INC.

Serenissima publications include digitally-enhanced reprints of authoritative editions for standard classical works, selected titles of lesser-known composers whose music deserves to be made available to a wider audience, and new editions updated to reflect the most recent findings of scholars and performers worldwide.

STUDY SCORES

BACH, Johann Sebastian (1685-1750)
MAGNIFICAT IN D, BWV 243 (NBA, ed. Dürr) SS-640

BEACH, Amy (1868-1944)
SYMPHONY IN E MINOR, Op. 32 "GAELIC" SS-063

CHADWICK, George Whitefield (1854-1931)
SYMPHONY NO. 2, Op. 21 .... SS-012
SYMPHONY NO. 3 in F SS-020

DEBUSSY, Claude Achille (1862-1918)
CHILDREN'S CORNER (orch. Caplet) SS-055
PETITE SUITE (orch. Büsser) SS-047

MACDOWELL, Edward (1861-1908)
SUITE NO. 2, Op. 48 "INDIAN" SS-470

MEDTNER, Nikolai (1880-1951)
PIANO CONCERTO NO. 1, Op. 33 .... SS-772

MUSSORGSKY, Modest (1839-1881)
PICTURES AT AN EXHIBITION, FOR WIND ORCHESTRA (orch. Simpson, ed. Reed) SS-101

RIMSKY-KORSAKOV, Nikolai (1844-1908)
SYMPHONY NO. 2, Op. 9 "ANTAR" (1897 version) SS-608

SIBELIUS, Jean (1865-1957)
SCENES HISTORIQUES, Opp. 25, 66 .... SS-659

STENHAMMAR, Wilhelm (1871-1927)
SERENADE, Op. 31 .... SS-004

STRAUSS, Johann II (1825-1899)
ROSES FROM THE SOUTH, Op. 388 (ed. McAlister) SS-624
WINE, WOMEN AND SONG, Op. 333 (ed. McAlister) SS-632

SUK, Josef (1874-1935)
FANTASICKE SCHERZO, Op. 25 .... SS-071
POHADKA LETA *(A SUMMER TALE)*, Op. 29 .... SS-594

TCHAIKOVSKY, Peter Ilich (1840-1893)
FRANCESCA DA RIMINI, Op. 32 .... SS-039
SWAN LAKE, BALLET IN FOUR ACTS, Op. 20 (ed. Simpson) SS-616
SWAN LAKE SUITE, Op. 20a (ed. Simpson) SS-314

VOCAL SCORES

BACH, Johann Sebastian (1685-1750)
CANATA NO. 4: "CHRIST LAG IN TODES BANDEN", BWV 4 .... Z2493
CANATA NO. 31: "DIE HIMMEL LACHT, DIE ERDE JUBILIERET", BWV 31 .... Z5156
CANATA NO. 79: "GOTT DER HERR IS SONN UND SCHILD", BWV 79 .... Z2515
CANATA NO. 129: "GELOBET SEI DER HERR, MEIN GOTT", BWV 129 .... Z8425
CANATA NO. 140: "WACHET AUF, RUFT UNS DIE STIMME", BWV 140 .... Z2530
CANATA NO. 150: "NACH DIR, HERR, VERLANGET MICH", BWV 150 (ed. Torvik) Z4521
CANATA NO. 191: "GLORIA IN EXCELSIS DEO", BWV 191 (ed. Torvik) Z7520
CHRISTMAS ORATORIO, BWV 248 .... Z2487
MAGNIFICAT IN D, BWV 243 (ed. Straube) Z2488

VOCAL SCORES - CONT.

VOCAL SCORES - CONT.

PURCELL, Henry (1659-1695)
DIDO & AENEAS, Z. 626 (arr. Cummings) Z2328

SAINT-SAENS, Camille (1835-1921)
ORATORIO DE NOEL, OP. 12 (arr. Gigout) Z2710

SCHUBERT, Franz Peter (1797-1828)
MASS IN G, D. 167 (arr. Spiro) Z2716
MASS IN E-FLAT, D. 950 (arr. Spengel) Z2718
STABAT MATER, D. 353 (arr. Gohler) Z2720

SCHUMANN, Robert (1810-1856)
REQUIEM, OP. 148 (arr. composer, ed. Torvik) Z7761

VIVALDI, Antonio (1678-1741)
CREDO, RV 591 (arr. Westermann) Z2734
GLORIA, RV 589 (arr. Westermann) Z2732
MAGNIFICAT, RV 610-611 (arr. Westermann) Z2733

www.ingramcontent.com/pod-product-compliance
Lightning Source LLC
Chambersburg PA
CBHW081543090426
42741CB00013BA/3243
* 9 7 8 1 9 3 2 4 1 9 2 2 1 *